The Unsung Heroes

The Unsung Heroes

by Nathan Aaseng

Lerner Publications Company
Minneapolis

To my grandparents

Page one: Johnnie Dunlop rides a bicycle with pneumatic tires, which his father, John Boyd Dunlop, invented in 1888.

Page two: One of the original McDonald's restaurants (shown here in 1949) was an octagonal stand in San Bernardino, California.

Library of Congress Cataloging-in-Publication Data

Aaseng, Nathan
  The unsung heroes/Nathan Aaseng.
    p. cm.
  Includes index.
    Summary: Introduces little-known individuals responsible for advancing well-known business products, including the originators of Coca-Cola, Hoover vacuum cleaners, and Bingo.
    ISBN 0-8225-0676-9
    1. Businessmen—Biography—Juvenile literature.
  [1. Businessmen.] I. Title.
  HC29.A247 1989
  388′.04′0922—dc19
  [B]
  [920]
                                                    88-3022
                                                      CIP
                                                      AC

Manufactured in the United States of America

2 3 4 5 6 7 8 9 10 99 98 97 96 95 94 93 92 91 90 89

Contents

The faces of Earl and Josephine Dickson might not be familiar to most people, but the product Earl Dickson invented—BAND-AID brand adhesive bandages—is well known. Dickson is one of the unsung heroes of the business world.

Introduction

MARRIAGE BROUGHT AN UNEXPECT-
ed danger to Josephine Dickson. She spent a good
share of her time in the kitchen of her New Bruns-
wick, New Jersey, home, where accidents seemed to
lurk behind every cupboard and counter. No sooner
did a knife nick on her finger heal than she would
get a small blister from picking up a hot pan or a
gouge from a potato peeler. She never required the
services of a doctor, but her injuries were painful.

Her husband, Earl, wished he could help. As a
cotton buyer in the purchasing department of the
Johnson & Johnson Company, he knew a lot about
medical supplies. His company was a pioneer in the
area of antiseptic (very clean) surgical dressings. But
he knew of no product designed to cover the kind of
minor wounds that were making his wife miserable.

7

After one of his wife's accidents, Dickson laid a strip of surgical tape made by Johnson & Johnson on the table with the adhesive side on top. Then he rolled up a pad of gauze and stuck it in the middle of the tape. Finally he covered the tape and gauze with a layer of crinoline, a light cotton fabric. From then on, whenever he or his wife suffered a cut or burn, they could snip off a piece of gauze-covered tape, remove the crinoline, and apply the tape to the wound.

Dickson's fellow employees at Johnson & Johnson thought the idea so clever that they urged him to show it to management. In 1920 he brought his handy medical dressing to company president James Johnson. Johnson was impressed. Soon the company began manufacturing a product patterned after Dickson's invention. The product was called the "BAND-AID." It soon became a part of nearly every first-aid kit in the U.S.

Early BAND-AID packages (top) *don't look much different than today's package* (bottom).

Dickson did not go totally unrewarded for his efforts. By the time of his retirement in 1957, he had become a vice-president of the company. But even though thousands of people depend on BAND-AID brand adhesive bandages every year, the inventor never became extremely wealthy or famous.

This book tells the little-known stories of some unsung heroes of the business world. These individuals created well-known businesses or products that changed our world. Their discoveries surround us; they are so commonplace that we take them for granted. We forget that at one time these products did not exist and that a real human being brought them into the world.

Few of these unsung heroes received even a fraction of the profits that others reaped from their efforts. The creators of some of the most popular products in the world died owning little more than the clothes on their backs.

Some of these creative people didn't realize the value of what they had invented. John Pemberton, who developed Coca-Cola® as a health drink, didn't recognize the worth of his product when he sold the rights to make it. Others knew the value of what they had but chose not to develop it. The McDonald brothers, builders of the famous fast-food restaurants, were simply not interested in seeking fame and fortune in the fast lane of big business. Still others fought hard to establish a profitable business but failed for a variety of reasons.

For every story in this book, there are undoubtedly many more stories of unknown and unrewarded individuals who helped shape a company or product. This book is a tribute to them as well as to those unsung heroes of business whose stories are told on the following pages.

A 1904 advertisement for COCA-COLA asserts that "men, women and children" are healthy and happy and drinking COCA-COLA because of its "delightful flavor and beneficial results." Early advertisements often linked the beverage to healthful qualities, since its inventor, John Styth Pemberton, created the drink as a kind of medicine. Later, COCA-COLA was promoted as a soft drink and only a soft drink.

Dr. Pemberton's Backyard Brew

COCA-COLA

COCA-COLA® HAS BEEN CALLED THE most familiar trademark in the world. The stylish lettering, curved bottle, and distinctive taste can be found anywhere from China to Australia. The giant Coca-Cola Company commands the largest retail sales force on earth and, next to the United States Postal Service, owns the largest fleet of trucks.

One would think that the person who dreamed up this popular product would have ranked among the wealthiest people on earth. No such luck for John Styth Pemberton. Although COCA-COLA has possibly created more millionaires than any other product, Pemberton himself made little money from his invention. He had originally developed COCA-COLA as a kind of medicine and had little success persuading people to buy it. It was not until after his death that the soft drink became the giant of the beverage industry.

Pemberton was a distinguished Confederate cavalry colonel who settled down in Atlanta, Georgia, to work as a pharmacist. During the 1880s, the drug industry was mostly a home remedy business. Each pharmacist developed his own tonics and medicines that would not only benefit the body, but would taste good as well. Pemberton brewed a number of home remedies over the years in a three-legged brass pot in his backyard. Among these was "French Wine Coca," his own version of a popular drink of the time. To make French Wine Coca, he steeped coca leaves in wine.

One hot day in early May of 1886, Pemberton boiled a new version of French Wine Coca in the kettle. This time he removed the wine and added an extract of the African kola nut. The coca leaves and the kola nuts were supposed to have a stimulating effect. Both, however, tasted very bitter. To make the drink palatable, Pemberton added plenty of sugar and a blend of flavors such as caramel, lime juice, nutmeg, cinnamon, and vanilla. When he sampled the mixture, Pemberton decided that this time he had really hit upon something.

Immediately he rushed over to Jacobs' Pharmacy, a popular Atlanta drugstore. Plunking a large jug on the counter, he asked the soda fountain manager, Willis Venable, to mix up a drink for him. One ounce of the syrup in the jug added to five

The beverage **industry** refers to the group of beverage manufacturers as a whole. The word *industry* can also be used more generally to mean all of a nation's manufacturing activity.

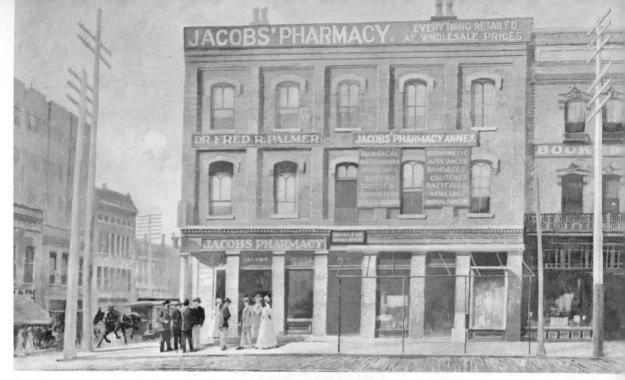

Pemberton tested his new beverage at Jacobs' Pharmacy in Atlanta.

ounces of water would make a delicious drink, he told Venable. Venable diluted the syrup as asked, and, along with Pemberton, tasted it. No doubt about it—Pemberton's syrup was delicious, certainly worth a second taste.

Then, according to legend, Venable made a careless mistake when he went to mix a second drink. Instead of adding plain water, the man added carbonated soda water. Venable apologized and was about to dump out the mistake when the men decided to taste the strange mixture. To their surprise, it was even better than the plain water version.

Pemberton soon began preparing to get his new drink on the market. He began selling to the public early in 1887. Few customers seemed eager to try the drink, however.

John Styth Pemberton sold the rights to make COCA-COLA for less than $2,000. Others who followed Pemberton made millions from the product.

For one thing, it was a difficult drink to describe. With so many ingredients, the flavor was not like anything else people had ever drunk, and people were hesitant to try something unusual. Pemberton handed out many free samples, but he made few sales. During the rest of 1887, Pemberton sold a total of 50 gallons of his syrup at one dollar per gallon. That was not even enough to cover advertising costs.

Several partners who supported Pemberton's

Advertising is the presentation of ideas, goods, and services to the public; it is paid for by a sponsor. Coca-Cola's advertising slogans, or themes, have changed many times over the years. Some of the Coca-Cola ad themes have been:

1886 Drink Coca-Cola
1906 The Great National Temperance Beverage
1922 Thirst knows no season
1929 The pause that refreshes
1938 The best friend thirst ever had
1948 Where there's Coke there's hospitality
1958 The cold, crisp taste of Coke
1963 Things go better with Coke
1970 It's the real thing
1979 Coke is It
1986 Catch the Wave

struggling new business suggested that the product needed a name. Pemberton had simply been pushing it as his "Nerve and Tonic Stimulant," a name that was not likely to attract reluctant customers. Combining the names of the two "medicinal" ingredients, coca leaves and kola nuts, the men coined the catchy name "COCA-COLA." Pemberton's bookkeeper, Frank Robinson, had a flair for calligraphy. With a few flourishing strokes of his pen, he wrote out the name in the fancy, flowing script that is still used to this day.

Pemberton continued to believe that what he was selling was a medicine, not a soft drink. He advertised that COCA-COLA could provide relief from headaches and hangovers and could help a person relax. The company's first color advertisement called the product a "Wonderful Brain and Nerve Tonic." Other advertising praised it as an "Esteemed Brain Tonic and Intellectual Beverage."

The public remained skeptical. COCA-COLA continued to sell so sluggishly that Pemberton decided it was not worth the effort of making it. Less than two years after introducing his product, John Pemberton sold all of his interests in COCA-COLA for $1,750.

Pemberton was not the only one who turned down the chance at a fortune. The two men who purchased the product rights from him in July of 1887 sold them five months later to two others. They, in turn, sold out to Atlanta druggist Asa Griggs Candler in 1891. It was Candler who first saw the potential of COCA-COLA. Gaining control of the company with an investment of $2,300, he organized the Coca-Cola Company and was clever enough to apply for trademark protection for the product. He also ordered that the COCA-COLA recipe be kept a secret, a policy that has been continued to this day.

Candler then began an advertising blitz, pouring out free samples and giving away coupons and souvenirs. Gradually sales of the soft drink began to increase. A big break came in 1894 when Joseph Biedenharn, a confectioner in Vicksburg,

The names *Coca-Cola* and *Coke* and the Coca-Cola lettering are all **trademarks**—words, names, symbols, or devices used by a manufacturer to identify its products and distinguish them from other products. Only the Coca-Cola Company can legally use the name Coca-Cola.

Asa Griggs Candler bought the Coca-Cola Company for a mere $2,300. In 1919 the company was sold for $25 million.

The COCA-COLA bottle used from 1894-1900 did not yet have the familiar curved shape.

Investing money in a business means giving money or something else of value to the business with the expectation of getting the money back with a little extra if the business is successful. Every new business requires an initial investment of some amount of money. It may be the money of the person starting the business, a loan from the bank, money from a group of investors, or a loan from a friend.

Mississippi, decided that instead of making the customer come to the product, he would take the product to the customer. A number of United States citizens had seen the introduction of bottled soft drinks in Cuba. It made sense to Biedenharn that a person working hard in a hot climate would be a perfect customer for a bottled soft drink. Biedenharn installed bottling machinery in the back of his store and began taking bottles of COCA-COLA to workers on plantations and at lumber camps along the Mississippi River.

Candler had always seen soft drinks made in drugstores by adding water to syrup, and he was originally opposed to the newfangled notion of bottling COCA-COLA. In 1899 he agreed to let someone else take a chance on that end of the business. He sold exclusive rights to bottle COCA-COLA to a pair of lawyers from Chattanooga, Tennessee. The lawyers, who had to borrow heavily to buy these rights, quickly made their investment pay off. Before long, COCA-COLA was being sold in the unique, gracefully curved bottle, advertised as "the container that goes anywhere."

The successes of the COCA-COLA manufacturer and the bottlers fed one another. While the Atlanta-based firm poured more than $1 million into advertising in 1911, bottlers made the product available across the country. Soon everyone connected with Pemberton's creation was growing rich.

Candler also severed ties with the old Pemberton

medicinal image. Advertisements no longer contained Pemberton's claims of healing. COCA-COLA was now a soft drink and nothing but a soft drink.

Naturally, many competitors were eager to take advantage of COCA-COLA's popularity. Candler's foresight in registering his product as a trademark helped stave off a wave of unscrupulous manufacturers. In 1916 courts outlawed such blatant copycat products as Koca-Nola, Koke, Cay-Ola, Cold Cola, and Coca. The only major battle the Coca-Cola Company lost was for the use of the word "cola," which eventually became the generic name for a soft drink flavor.

By 1919 COCA-COLA was selling more than 20 million gallons of syrup per year. At that time it was sold for $25 million to Atlanta banker Ernest Woodruff and an investor group he had organized. The company has continued to grow into a giant organization, and COCA-COLA is sold around the world. Today, every thirsty person who opens a can or a bottle of COCA-COLA owes thanks to John Styth Pemberton. His creation of a backyard brew unintentionally turned out to be an act of charity.

Competition is one of the basic features of the U.S. business system. **Competition** means trying to get something that others are also trying to get. Competition in business can occur in many ways. Producers compete for the best raw materials. Businesses compete with each other for the most customers. One way to do this is by selling a product at a lower price than other manufacturers. Another way is to provide some other kind of advantage. A candy store might give away free samples to customers, for example.

Wheel of Fortune

Dunlop

John Boyd Dunlop

IT IS GENERALLY AGREED THAT THE invention of the wheel was one of the most important technological advances of all time. Certainly humankind owes a debt beyond measure to its anonymous inventor. The wheel, however, was only a start. The automobile industry could not have gone far riding along on wheels; it needed tires.

Tires can be made so well and so cheaply today that they are only a minor consideration for most consumers shopping for automobiles and bicycles. Seventy years ago, however, the cost of tires made up a fourth of the entire purchase price of a new car. The expense of replacing the tires, which wore out quickly, plus the jaw-cracking experience of riding in vehicles with tires made of solid rubber, made people appreciative of the worth of a good tire.

Some of those who worked the hardest to put tires on solid footing received little better reward for their work than did the unknown inventor of the wheel. Charles Goodyear died penniless, even though he discovered a process that made shock-absorbing rubber more suitable for use in tires. The inventor of the first pneumatic tire was ignored, and his discovery had to be invented all over again more than 40 years later!

A pneumatic tire is one that is filled with a tube of air for a shock cushion. Robert W. Thomson, a 23-year-old Scottish civil engineer, invented the first one nearly 150 years ago. He wrapped a rubberized tube filled with air in a strip of leather. This tube was then stretched around a metal tire on his bicycle and fastened securely to the metal with bolts. Buoyed by this kind of cushion, his bicycle rode very smoothly, and Thomson recognized his idea as one worth patenting. England granted him a patent in 1845, and the United States followed suit two years later.

Robert W. Thomson

But Thomson was far ahead of his time. He couldn't generate enough interest in his tires to make it worthwhile to produce them. Possibly the fastening method—which required 70 bolts—discouraged people from taking his invention seriously.

It wasn't until 1888 that someone else took a careful look at the possibilities for the pneumatic tire. Another Scotsman, John Boyd Dunlop, independently devised a similar invention. Dunlop,

*Dunlop's new pneumatic tires were put to the test in a bicycle race—
and they won.*

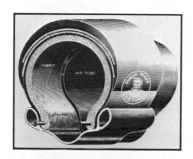

*A cutaway diagram of a
1900 Dunlop car tire*

a veterinary surgeon who practiced in Belfast, Ireland, bought a tricycle for his 10-year-old son. But the jolting ride of the solid rubber wheels over the cobblestone streets took some of the fun out of the toy. Seeking a way to get a more pleasant ride, Dunlop took apart a soft garden hose to use as a tube. Like Thomson, he wrapped the air-filled rubber tube in coarser material—in this case canvas, or Irish linen. Unlike Thomson, he used an adhesive, rather than bolts, to cement the tire to the metal wheel.

A year later, he demonstrated this new tire to a hooting audience at a Belfast cycle track. Most of the contestants in the bicycle race rode the standard equipment for the time—an enormous wheel of solid rubber in the front, with a tiny wheel at the rear. In the middle of this pack of bicycles rode one contestant on a steel bicycle supported only by two small, identical wheels. The crowd's laughter turned to startled cheers, however, when the oddly designed bicycle easily won the race.

The secret of its success did not lie in the size of the tires, but in their design. Dunlop's pneumatic tires simply traveled over the ground much more smoothly than the solid rubber wheels.

With the value of his invention so clearly demonstrated, Dunlop's newly obtained patent was potentially valuable. Dunlop, however, did not care to gamble his hard-earned veterinary career on a chance discovery. The bushy-bearded doctor sold the rights to his invention for a small sum of money so that he could continue to concentrate on his chosen profession. William Bowden, who bought the rights, sold them off just as quickly to an Irish bicycle racer named W.H. DuCros.

With firsthand knowledge of the tire's superiority, DuCros believed it was worth the risk of starting a new business, and he organized the Pneumatic Tyre Company, Ltd. Although Dr. Dunlop had nothing more to do with the invention, "Dunlop" was added to the company's name to identify the tires as the kind that Dunlop had invented.

Unlike Thomson's invention, this pneumatic tire did more than attract dust in a garage. In 1891 the Hartford Rubber Works began manufacturing the

A **patent** is the exclusive right to own, use, and dispose of an invention. If you invent a machine or a device, you may apply for a patent. The U.S. Patent Office issues more than 1,200 patents each week. Patents for inventions are granted to the owner for 17 years; then the patent expires.

The word **manufacturing** refers to the making of articles by hand or with machines. The word **production** refers to all activities involved in converting natural resources, such as iron or trees, into finished goods, or products, such as plows or wood or paper.

A branch of the British Dunlop Corp. in Bombay, India, in 1889

To **license** an invention is to authorize another person's (or company's) use of the invention for a fee. Patent rights can also be sold outright, as Dunlop did.

tire in the United States under license from the British firm. By the turn of the century, automobile makers as well as bicycle enthusiasts saw the worth of Dunlop's invention. With further improvements, such as the use of clinches to fasten the inner tube to the rim, the pneumatic tire transformed the car from an unreliable rattletrap to a vital means of transportation.

While the pneumatic tire helped usher in the era of the automobile, for John Dunlop there was no benefit to being involved in the birth of the tire industry. Although the name of Dunlop lives on in tire manufacturing, the inventor never received more than a token payment for his efforts.

The Giant
That Left Its
Masters Behind

General Motors

THE SUCCESS OF THE FORD MOTOR Company in the marketplace, while impressive, has not begun to compare with its success in the history books. Most people realize that the person behind Ford automobiles was a self-made man named Henry Ford. The story of how he perfected the automobile assembly line and cranked out his inexpensive Model T has made him one of the most well-known pioneers of industry.

Meanwhile, millions of people drive Buicks and Chevrolets with no idea of what those names mean. General Motors—of which the Buick and Chevrolet divisions are only a part—has far surpassed Ford in sales and has become the largest company in the world. Its image is that of a faceless bureaucracy. The names of the founders of GM faded quickly into obscurity. Yet Will Durant, David Buick, and Louis Chevrolet each played a key role in creating an automobile empire so large that it affects nearly everyone in the Western world. This is the story of how these three men were left in the dust by their own creation.

Buick Bathtubs

The name Buick is not usually associated with bathtubs, but David Dunbar Buick made his fortune in the bathtub business. Born in Scotland in 1855, he moved with his family to Detroit, Michigan, as an infant. His parents died three years later. As a teenager, he left school to work at a plumbing supply company. When the business went bankrupt, Buick and a friend bought the defunct company, which they renamed Buick and Sherwood Manufacturing Company. They quickly worked to make it profitable.

Had Buick stuck to making plumbing fixtures, he would have retired a wealthy man. But, like many businessmen of his time, he fell under the spell of the revolutionary "horseless carriage." The field wasn't completely new to him. A gifted inventor, he had dabbled in small engines and had developed a gas motor. Just before the turn of the century, he became convinced that there was a demand for a good automobile. Selling his bath supply business for about $100,000 in 1898, he began to think about ways of putting an engine on wheels.

Buick set to work in 1900 and formed a company

A company is said to make a **profit** when the money it earns from sales amounts to more than the cost of producing the goods or service.

A basic rule of business involves supply and demand. The number of products that are offered for sale at different prices at a certain time is called **supply.** **Demand** is the number of products that people are willing to buy at different prices at a certain time. In general, the greater the demand for a product, the higher the price can be set.

David Buick

If you are in **debt**, it means that you owe someone something. Debt is an obligation to pay something. A company or individual goes into **bankruptcy** when they cannot pay their debts.

called Buick Auto-Vim and Power. Skilled at attracting dynamic young engineers, Buick made his Detroit firm a laboratory for testing new concepts in automotives. One of these was the "valve-in-head" motor, which involved a new placement of the air-intake and exhaust-outlet valves. This design innovation improved the efficiency of the Buick engine so much that it was copied by all automakers. David Buick personally designed most of the motor, the chassis, and many of the body parts of his new car.

Unfortunately, the company—which eventually became known as the Buick Motor Company—had trouble translating ideas into action. In 1903 Buick had nothing to show for his efforts except an experimental model, and most of his plans were still on the drawing board.

By this time, Buick had used up most of the money he had made in the plumbing business. He turned to two wealthy friends, who reorganized the company. Soon, however, Buick's new company was draining his friends' checking accounts dry. The company was on the edge of bankruptcy when the Flint Wagon Works came to the rescue and bought it. But the wagon works' president, James Whiting, had no interest in cars. He had bought the company for its engine, which he thought would be useful for farm equipment.

David Buick wasn't ready to give up, though. He persuaded his new boss to let him build a two-cylinder car he had designed. When the car rolled

David Buick's first automobile was built in 1903.

out of the factory, it seemed that Buick's work had finally paid off. Test-driven by Buick's son, it raced over 115 miles of rutted roads from Flint to Detroit in just over three and a half hours. Auto experts agreed that Buick had built an excellent car with the most powerful automobile engine ever made.

Buick's victory, however, came after the battle was already lost. In 1904 the United States automobile market was chaotic. In 1899 there had been about 100 companies building cars, and only one of them had made as many as 200 vehicles. For the next few years, anywhere from 40 to 60 new models of cars were being rushed into production each year. Many of the companies went out of business the same year they introduced their product. Customers knew little about the models on the market and could not determine which were good cars. Despite the Buick's proven quality, only a handful of them were sold during 1904.

James Whiting quickly saw that it would take more money than he could afford—well over a million dollars—to keep the Buick Motor Company afloat. When he found a buyer for the company late in 1904, he eagerly sold out. David Buick, who had long since lost both his fortune and control of the company, was soon out of the picture altogether. In 1906 he severed his last ties with the company he had founded. At the time of his death in 1929, David Dunbar Buick was scratching out a bare living as a clerk at a vocational school in Detroit.

Durant—Easy Come, Easy Go

The man who bought the Buick Motor Company was James Whiting's main competitor in the wagon business, William Crapo Durant. Born in Boston, Massachusetts, in 1861, Durant moved with his family to Flint, Michigan, where his grandfather had made a fortune in the lumber business. Will went to work in the family lumberyard at the age of 16. He began to dream of building a business of his own.

Durant made his move on impulse in 1886 when a friend offered him a ride in his new two-wheeled cart. Learning that the sturdy, newly patented wagon came from nearby Coldwater, Michigan, he went there to tour the facilities. By the time he finished

William C. Durant, president of GM from 1916 to 1920, built the company into an important force in the automobile industry. Durant's business gambles led to his downfall, however.

his inspection, Durant was reaching for his money. At age 25, he became the primary owner of the Coldwater Road Cart Company, later renamed the Durant-Dort Carriage Company.

Durant's confidence and soft-spoken charm earned him praise as the "greatest salesman in the country." His persuasive skills, along with his strategy of relentless expansion and aggressive marketing, pushed Durant-Dort into a position as the number one carriage maker in the United States by 1904.

At the time, Durant was skeptical of the new horseless carriages. He was sure that most people would be unwilling to put up with the loud engine noise. His opinion changed, however, thanks to another fateful test drive. In 1904 Durant was given a ride in the new Buick. Not only was it quiet, but its quality and style were impressive. Just as before, a test drive led to a sale. With the noise problem eased, Durant

Marketing is the process of developing a product, determining how much it should cost, deciding how it should be sold, and making sure that people who want to buy the product can get it. One slogan describes marketing as "finding a need and filling it."

By getting loans, Durant was making use of credit, a major part of the U.S. business system. **Credit** is the ability to get goods or services in exchange for a promise to pay later. A popular way of describing credit is the saying "Buy now, pay later." Banks play an important role in the credit system. People place the money they have saved in a bank. The bank pays the person **interest**, a payment for the use of the person's money. The bank then loans money to businesses, which eventually pay back the money plus an interest payment.

Durant was forced to sell shares, or portions, of GM stock. A **stock** is a small part of ownership in a company. Ownership is divided among many shareholders or owners. Stocks are traded—bought and sold—in stock exchanges. The most well known stock exchange is on Wall Street in New York City.

now believed that the automobile was the transportation of the future. He eagerly took over the floundering Buick Motor Company.

Durant worked 18 to 20 hours a day building his automobile empire. He poured $1.5 million into production facilities and hired top drivers to form a Buick racing team to promote the product. Within four years, Durant had made the tiny Buick company the leader of the automobile industry. In 1908 Buick outsold Ford, 8,847 cars to 6,181.

What might have been a milestone for other people was just a stepping-stone for empire-builder Durant. His next move was to buy a number of top automobile companies. In 1908 he obtained two plums, Cadillac and Oldsmobile, and merged them with Buick into an organization called General Motors. Meanwhile, Durant put together a national sales organization, built plants, and bought firms that made parts such as gears and transmissions.

These investments required a great deal more money than Durant had, but it was easy for him to get loans. As long as business was booming—and Durant saw no reason why it should slow down—General Motors could pay off the loans and keep growing. Durant miscalculated, however. During a business slump in 1910, he ran out of cash to pay his suppliers and his lenders. In order to save the company, Durant had to sell his shares of GM stock.

Durant's dream of an empire was far from over, though. With profits from his General Motors stock, he acquired control of the Little Motor Company. Durant then joined forces with another small car company, which was started by one of his former employees, Louis Chevrolet.

The Dashing Race Driver

Louis Chevrolet was born in 1878, the son of a poor Swiss watchmaker. Growing up in France, Chevrolet showed an early genius for mechanics. While in his teens, he invented a wine pump that became widely used in the industry. He next traveled across the Atlantic Ocean to seek greater adventure. Soon Chevrolet entered an automobile race at New York's Morris Park. It was a lucky break for an amateur like Chevrolet to test his skill against a field of top racers that included the legendary Barney Oldfield and Walter Christie. But Chevrolet left his more famous rivals in the dust.

A large, powerful man with a flowing mustache and a fearless racing style, Louis Chevrolet became a star on the racing circuit. In 1907 Will Durant hired him for his successful Buick racing team. In a 158-mile race in Massachusetts in 1909, Chevrolet finished a full 20 minutes ahead of the runner-up! Durant and Chevrolet became friends.

When Durant was forced to leave General Motors, Chevrolet decided to support him by leaving as well. It was the perfect time to test his ideas for improving the automobile. His ambitious goal was to make an automobile that combined stylish looks

The first Chevrolet automobile, produced in 1912. Louis Chevrolet is shown standing, left, without a hat.

with power and increased reliability and sell it at a moderate price.

In 1911 the Chevrolet Motor Company was organized. Chevrolet did not achieve all his goals. His

Construction began on the huge General Motors Building in Detroit in 1920. The building is still a Detroit landmark.

first model was a large, powerful, six-cylinder car that sold for $2,150, not exactly a moderate price at the time. Nonetheless, the company sold almost 3,000 cars in its first year of production.

When Chevrolet and Durant joined forces, the magic of Chevrolet's famous name and the marketing expertise of his old boss combined to overcome the problems that were sinking other car companies. The Chevrolet Motor Company sold every car it made in 1914.

Lightning Strikes Twice

Chevrolet's success enabled Durant to form a complicated scheme to regain control of General Motors. Backed by powerful, wealthy friends, Durant secretly began purchasing shares of GM stock. He then traded shares of his suddenly attractive Chevrolet stock for GM stock. As a result of this complex financial maneuver, the giant General Motors was taken over by Durant and the little Chevrolet Motor Company.

After merging Chevrolet with General Motors in 1918, Durant returned to his tactic of rapid expansion. What he couldn't build, he bought, and what he couldn't buy, he borrowed. In 1916 he purchased companies that made horns, bearings, and ignition systems.

General Motors products had to sell well to keep up with the company's expenses. Just as in 1910, consumer demand dropped far below expectations,

A large company like GM is often divided into several different units called **divisions**. Most businesses start small. The owner makes most decisions and performs most tasks. As the company grows, different activities are assigned to different people. Gradually, different activities are performed in separate areas called departments. If the department continues to grow, it may become a separate division.

One of the companies acquired by Durant was Fisher Body. Workers varnished cars there in this 1918 photograph.

and Durant and General Motors were caught off guard. Uneasy investors tried to pull out the money they had invested in the company. On July 20, 1920, more than 100,000 shares of GM stock were sold on the stock market by panicky investors, causing the value of the stock to drop dramatically.

This placed Durant in a ticklish spot. Suddenly all of Durant's friends who had invested their savings in his company were in danger of losing their money. To help them, Durant kept buying up the stock that nobody wanted. He hoped that he could prop up the price of the stock so that his friends could get a reasonable price when they sold it.

Durant bought enough stock to save his friends' investments, but he couldn't save himself. Within a few months, Durant's personal fortune of $100 million had vanished and he was deeply in debt.

No Happy Endings

That was the end of Durant's career at General Motors. Others, particularly Alfred P. Sloan, president of GM from 1923-37, steered the company out of the Depression and on to fantastic growth. But Will Durant never recovered. His final effort in the automotive world was to form Durant Motors, Inc., in 1921. But the business was dissolved in 1933. Two years later, the once-powerful auto empire-builder filed for bankruptcy. His debts were listed as $2 million; his only belongings were $250 worth of clothes.

Durant tried twice more to get back on his feet. Neither effort worked out, however, and when he died in 1947, Will Durant was penniless.

Louis Chevrolet did not fare much better than Durant. After the initial success of the Chevrolet in 1913, Durant had put the Chevrolet name on a smaller, inexpensive car. Louis had been furious at the thought of a "cheap" car carrying his respected name. He had wanted nothing more to do with Durant's enterprise and had sold his holdings for a small amount. Had he waited a few more years, until Chevrolet's stock was worth much more, he could have received many times what he was given.

Following his departure from his namesake company, Louis had designed the cars that finished first at the Indianapolis 500 race in both 1920 and 1921. But soon after, his career had fallen apart. Attempts to design and sell new automobiles and airplanes failed.

After working for General Motors as a consultant for a few years, the mechanical wizard who lent his name to the largest-selling car division in history died of cerebral hemorrhage in 1941.

Ironically, the company that now rings up roughly $100 billion in sales each year did not bring wealth to three of the men who built it up from the ground.

The Sickly Janitor

Hoover Vacuum Cleaners

Hoover's first vacuum cleaner, introduced in 1908. At that time, the company's name was the Electric Suction Sweeper Company.

For MANY YEARS, THE NAME HOOVER so dominated the vacuum cleaner business that many people referred to their carpet cleaner as a "Hoover," regardless of what company made it. If fate had been a little more sentimental, however, the cleaner might have become known as a "Spangler." After all, it was a sickly janitor named James Murray Spangler who in 1907 invented the machine that launched the W.H. Hoover Company on the road to fame.

Spangler was a tinkerer who had spent most of his life trying to invent something worthwhile and profitable. After many years, he had little to show for his efforts, other than ruined health and a mound of debts. Dreams of glory had dissolved into a dreary life of pure survival. To pay his bills, Spangler took a job as a janitor in a department store in Canton, Ohio.

He quickly discovered that cleaning carpets was hazardous to his health. Although suction-type carpet sweepers had been invented as early as 1859, they were not practical. In Spangler's time they were ponderous and bulky and hard to manueuver. Worse yet, the cleaner kicked up clouds of dust and dirt. With breathing already difficult for him because of a chronic lung condition, Spangler was thrown into fits of coughing and wheezing.

Even though his job was killing him, Spangler was so desperately in need of money that he could not afford to quit. Instead, he used his inventing skills to design a clean, portable carpet cleaner. Lacking the money to order custom-made parts, the janitor fashioned a homemade contraption from the scraps available to him. Rescuing an old soap-box from a trash heap, he sealed the cracks with tape and mounted the box on a small set of wheels. At one end of the box, he attached a roller brush from the store's carpet sweeper. He then connected the brush to a small electric motor. Finally he sealed off the other end of the box with a pillowcase.

James Murray Spangler

Powered by the motor, the roller brush swept up dirt from the carpet. The suction effect of the motor then funneled the dirt to the back of the machine, where it was collected in the pillowcase.

Not only did Spangler's "electric suction sweeper" save his health, but it also seemed a promising way out of his financial troubles. He knew what a work-saver his invention was, and he was sure others

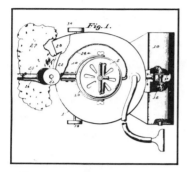

***Patent illustration for
Spangler's sweeper***

Hoover knew that saddles
and other horse-related
goods were becoming obso-
lete. An **obsolete** product or
process is no longer used
because a new and better
product or process—such as
the automobile, in Hoover's
case—has replaced it.

would see the benefit as well. While applying for a
patent in 1908, he organized a company to manufacture and sell the electric sweepers. But a new business
venture usually takes time and money, and the ill,
debt-ridden man had neither time nor money.

During his brief struggle to get his company off
the ground, Spangler demonstrated one of his
machines to his cousin-in-law, Susan Hoover. It was
a good move, for not only did Hoover buy it, but
she happened to be married to the influential mayor
of North Canton, Ohio (then New Berlin), who was
looking to launch a new type of business.

When he first inspected Spangler's invention,
William H. Hoover was nearly 60 years old. The
tannery that he had bought from his father and
run for over 35 years employed more than 200
workers. For more than 100 years, the Hoover business had made most of its money on saddles, horse
collars, and harnesses. Hoover realized, though, that
the tannery's entire line of goods was on the verge
of becoming obsolete. The sudden emergence of
the automobile at the turn of the century threat-
ened to throw every saddlemaker in the country
out of business.

It would have been easy for the well-to-do busi-
nessman to retire and admit that the times had
passed him by, or he could have joined the many
horse owners who tried to prevent the advance of
the "horseless carriage." But William Hoover showed
an ability to adapt to the times. He looked for other

ways to stay in business. While continuing to make his original products, Hoover kept his factory in full operation by branching out into straps and belts for car engines. Realizing that this was just a stopgap measure, he also kept his eyes open for new manufacturing possibilities.

When he saw the electric suction sweeper, he decided it was just what he was looking for. More and more houses were being served by electricity, and Hoover foresaw that demand for an electric sweeper would grow with the use of electricity. After some negotiation, he reached an agreement with Spangler in 1908. Hoover agreed to pay all of Spangler's debts and to hire the inventor as product supervisor. Spangler would also receive a salary based on the number of sweepers sold. In exchange, Spangler signed over the newly issued patent rights to the invention to Hoover.

Hoover started the Electric Suction Sweeper Company in a corner of his leather goods factory. With three men working to produce five or six sweepers a day, Hoover was ready to put his new product on the market within three months of his deal with Spangler.

The experienced Hoover found a clever method of solving the problems that Spangler had faced in trying to attract customers. He placed a magazine advertisement announcing that his company would offer a free 10-day trial to anyone who answered the ad. Then, instead of sending electric suction

William H. Hoover

Hoover sent vacuum cleaners to store owners to use as demonstrator models if the customers didn't buy them.

sweepers directly to the customers who answered the ad, he wrote to them and told them that they could pick up the sweeper at a local store. In the meantime, he shipped his product to the store owner. Along with it, he included a letter instructing the store owner simply to collect the money and keep the sales commission if the customer was satisfied. If the customer returned the sweeper, the merchant could keep it as a demonstrator model.

The store owner could not lose. With his generous and wise offer, Hoover managed to create dealerships out of otherwise skeptical merchants. In its first year of operation, the company sold 372 electric suction sweepers.

After further improvements had been made to the sweeper, Hoover's 1912 sales reached nearly 4,000. By 1919 the business had grown so large that William Hoover dropped the leather goods business that had been part of his family for more than a century to concentrate on vacuum cleaners. Switching his sales strategy to a network of demonstrators, Hoover's company was instrumental in bringing vacuum cleaners into widespread use in the home.

James Spangler received the satisfaction of knowing that he had at last invented something useful. But other than freeing himself from the worry of paying off creditors, he was not able to share in the success of his brainstorm. Spangler died in 1915, without profiting from the success that his machine would enjoy nationwide. In 1910 the Electric Suction Sweeper Company was renamed the W.H. Hoover Company. So it was that Hoover, not Spangler, became the name that meant "vacuum cleaner."

A **dealership** is a store or other sales agency which is authorized by a company such as Hoover to sell its product.

Game
Without an Owner

Bingo

THE GAME IS SO SIMPLE, SO COMMON, and so much a part of life in the United States that it's hard to imagine it ever had a beginning. Bingo seems like a part of Western cultural heritage that has been passed along from generation to generation.

Surprisingly, bingo has been around a relatively short time, and its popularity can be traced to two individuals. Considering the amount of money spent on bingo each year, one might expect that these men amassed a fortune. But the man who formulated the game in its present form used it only as a carnival attraction. His name has been forgotten and even the title of his game discarded. The man who borrowed the idea from him, Edwin S. Lowe, did well in the game business, but his name is rarely associated with his most popular game. Almost

Bingo—or beano, as it was called—began as a carnival game. Edwin Lowe discovered the game at a Georgia carnival in 1929.

immediately after Lowe introduced it, bingo became a game without an owner. Anyone who wanted to manufacture the game was free to do so.

The bingo story started with an unknown carnival pitchman, or caller, from the United States. Looking for a way to keep his children occupied while he traveled with a carnival in Europe, the caller bought them a popular game known as Lotto. Lotto had been played in Europe since the 16th century. The game, which had many variations, involved random selection of numbers and letters to fill up squares on a board. The pitchman's children enjoyed it so much that he wondered if he

During the 1930s, the United States suffered through a period called the **Great Depression**. In general, a depression is a period when production and consumption of goods and services slow down. It is a time marked by unemployment and business failures, and people do not have much money to live on.

The Great Depression of the 1930s followed the stock market crash of 1929. Economic growth in the 1920s had led many Americans to invest in stocks. The value of stocks had soared as more and more people invested, but in late October, 1929, stock prices had dropped. Investors had panicked and sold stocks frantically. The "crash," as it was called, had resulted in drastically lowered stock prices.

The crash helped trigger the Great Depression. Following the crash, banks stopped giving many loans to businesses, and businesses cut back production. Millions of people lost their jobs, and poverty spread throughout the United States. By the early 1930s, the U.S. economy was paralyzed. At the height of the Depression, in 1933, about 13 million Americans were out of work. The Depression continued until 1941, when the U.S. entered World War II.

could use some form of it in the carnival. Eventually he designed a game which he called beano and tried it out on European audiences. The crowds seemed fascinated. Beano was firmly established as a carnival money-maker by the time the show returned to the United States in 1929.

The country was reeling then from the first effects of the devastating Great Depression. One of those caught in the despair was a toy salesman named Edwin S. Lowe. Lowe could not quite scrape together survival money from his sales commissions, so he tried to branch into a small business of manufacturing games to earn extra money. People were no more willing to spend money for games than for toys, though. After a fruitless sales trip to Atlanta, Georgia, Lowe fought off his discouragement, climbed into his car, and set off toward his next appointment in Jacksonville, Florida.

While driving late at night, he was dazzled by the glare of bright lights along the highway. Stopping to investigate, he found a carnival set up on the edge of a small town in Georgia. It seemed late for a carnival to be running. Lowe soon discovered that the carnival was trying to close up for the night. All the booths were shut down except one, and that booth was swarming with enthusiastic people who refused to go home.

Despite the late hour, Lowe's curiosity was piqued, and he joined the crowd. A caller barked out numbers, and several tables full of players listened eagerly and covered spaces on a game board with beans. Whenever a player filled in a row of numbers on the card, he or she called out "Beano" and was awarded a prize. Being in the game business, Lowe was intrigued enough to dig out the nickel that it cost to enter the game, but he could find no one willing to give up a seat. Although the pitchman wearily begged the players to leave, the crowd was not finally chased out until 3:00 A.M.

Lowe thought about manufacturing a boxed version of the game. But he did not trust what he had witnessed. He wondered if a group of party-goers had caused all the fuss. As an experiment, he adapted the game for home use and invited some friends over for the evening. To his surprise and delight, his guests acted as eager and uninhibited as those at the carnival. The party dragged on into the early hours of morning and still the guests refused to leave. By the time he finally hustled them off to bed, they had begun playing for money.

One woman was so flushed with excitement upon winning a game that she forgot what she was supposed to say. After stuttering for a few moments, she blurted out "Bingo!" As soon as he heard the word, Lowe decided that it was a better name for the game than beano.

Lowe began manufacturing bingo in two variations—a 12-card set for one dollar and a 24-card set for two dollars. At the time, Lowe was selling three other games without much success. But no sooner did his bingo hit the market than it was snatched up by eager customers. Orders began pouring in. Before long, many competitors hoping to get rich on Lowe's idea were making and selling bingo games. Although

Many different companies began manufacturing bingo.

Today bingo is often played as a fund-raiser at churches and other organizations.

Lowe could have protected the name "bingo" under trademark laws, Lowe decided not to. Since he was already swamped with more orders than he could fill, he saw no reason to spend time in court fighting off imitators. Instead, he agreed to let his competitors use the name bingo for one dollar a year.

A short time later, Lowe was approached by a priest at Wilkes-Barre, Pennsylvania. The parish was in desperate need of money, and a woman had suggested using bingo to raise funds. The idea proved popular but also very expensive. Since the game had only 24 basic cards, there were many winners each time. The church had been forced to give out too many prizes. The priest needed more cards with more combinations of letters and numbers. Lowe took the problem to a mathematics professor at Columbia University and asked him to design 6,000 new cards, each of which would have a different combination of numbers. This was no simple task in the era before computers. The closer the man came to the goal of 6,000, the harder the task became. Lowe offered him more and more money per card until the goal was finally reached.

With the room for expansion provided by these new combinations, more than 10,000 bingo fund-raisers were played weekly in the United States in 1934. The game's popularity continued to grow. To this day, it remains a mainstay of fund-raising among nonprofit organizations.

While Lowe let go of control of his game, he fared much better than did the other key actor in the story. It is not known what became of the inventor of the carnival game beano. Whatever his fate, he was the ultimate unsung hero in a game enjoyed by millions.

A **nonprofit organization** is one which does not seek to make a profit. Some nonprofit organizations include the government, churches, schools, charities, and hospitals.

The Neglected Parents

Superman

SUPERMAN, THE LEGENDARY DEFENDer of truth, justice, and the American way, was originally designed as a symbol for everything that was good about the United States. Some of the shine was rubbed off his bright blue tights and red cape in an article published in 1975 in the *New York Times*, however. Given the "justice" dealt Superman's creators, the comic strip character could also be seen as a symbol of corporate power.

Superman originated not on the planet Krypton, but in Cleveland, Ohio. The year was 1932, and the United States was in the middle of the paralyzing Great Depression. But the bleak economic environment did not daunt the spirits of two 17-year-old Cleveland high school students. Jerry Siegel was determined to forge a career as a writer, and his friend Joe Shuster wanted to make his mark in the field of art. Both young men fed their imaginations by reading science fiction magazines. Impatient to get on with their careers, they began to create stories and publish them in their own magazine, which they called *Science Fiction*.

Siegel wrote one story about an evil scientist. "Reign of the Superman" was inspired by the acrobatic feats of one of his favorite movie actors, Douglas Fairbanks, Jr. It is hard to imagine now, but in the 1930s, "super" was not a common part of people's vocabulary. Siegel chose the name Superman because it sounded authoritative. Shuster added illustrations and the story appeared in the boys' *Science Fiction* magazine in 1933. The two began toying with the idea of making a comic strip out of it.

Neither had a clear idea of how to do that until the summer of 1934. Kept awake one night by a muggy July heat wave, Siegel let his thoughts wander. He thought of ways to improve the Superman character. By morning, he had so fleshed out his new character that he was ready for Shuster to begin drawing immediately. The new Superman was a heroic, almost invincible character fighting to preserve the ideals of the United States. In a time of hardship for most Americans, Siegel hoped the character might boost people's spirits.

His ideas borrowed heavily from much science fiction of the time, particularly a novel entitled *Gladiator* by Philip Wylie. Siegel decided that his

Jerry Siegel

Joe Shuster

A news **syndicate** is an organization that sells materials for publication in several newspapers at the same time.

character would be dressed in a colorful, tight-fitting costume. Born on another planet, he would come to earth and become a powerful defender of freedom and justice. He would maintain his privacy by living a normal life as an ordinary person, revealing his secret identity to no one.

After Shuster had completed the artwork, the two tried to sell their comic strip. Most news syndicates turned them down altogether. A few expressed interest but called for changes that Siegel and Shuster were unwilling to make.

Frustrated about their failure to sell the Superman concept, the two boys turned to other comic book stories to earn a living. They sold two features, "Slam Bradley" and "Spy," to a comic book publisher named Harry Donenfield. In 1938 Donenfield

Superman's success inspired a league of other superheroes, such as Batman. (© 1988 DC Comics Inc.)

Opposite: A 50th anniversary edition of the first Action Comics cover to feature Superman (© 1988 DC Comics Inc.)

was looking for a character for a comic series he was starting called Action Comics. He asked the advice of M.C. Gaines, who was considered one of the top authorities on comic books. Gaines recommended Siegel and Shuster's Superman.

After more than four years of discouragement, the two young men had found a buyer. In June 1938, the Superman comic strip first appeared on newsstands. The response was overwhelming. Before long Superman was the most popular comic character in the country. Superman radio and television series were started, followed by cartoon shows and movies. Not only did Superman ensure the success of Action Comics, but it provided a boost for the entire comic book industry. Leagues of superheroes followed Superman to enchant youngsters for generations.

Since publishers and producers have made millions of dollars from the Superman character, one would think that Siegel and Shuster became millionaires at a young age. But they were too inexperienced to know what rights they had and how to protect them. The men sold the rights to the character of Superman to their employer for a small amount of money. For a few years, they produced all the work on the Superman strip for Action Comics for about $15 per page. After a few years, however, Shuster's eyesight began to fail, and the two young men were replaced by other, more polished artists.

Siegel and Shuster sued to regain control of their creation and to receive a share of the enormous profits that others were reaping. Although they earned some money from Superman products, they didn't win back the rights they had naively sold.

While Superman enjoyed celebrity status, his two creators fell into poverty. Shuster's eyesight was so poor that he could get only low-paying manual jobs. Legally blind, he lived in a threadbare New York City apartment. Nearly 40 years after he had drawn the first pictures of Superman for the world, he had to depend on a brother to help him pay his bills. At the same time, 61-year-old Jerry Siegel was working as a poorly paid clerk for the state of California. Although he had continued to write for D.C. Comics (owner of Action Comics) until the late 1960s, his financial situation had become so desperate that he had once sold his precious collection of old comic books to make some money.

Over the years, the two men had fought for a share of the Superman profits. At last they admitted defeat and, in 1975, they turned to newspapers to publicize the injustice of their situation. Shortly after a news conference they held—at which they were supported by cartoonists throughout the country—they obtained a settlement. The owners of the Superman rights agreed to pay each of the creators of Superman a pension for the rest of their lives.

While the money offered desperately needed

A **pension** is a fixed sum of money paid regularly to someone.

The 1978 movie Superman *starred Christopher Reeve in the title role.*

comfort to the two men, it was still just a tiny percentage of what others had made from Superman, and it was more than 30 years late in coming. Superman had gone on to fame and fortune. But he left his parents behind.

Sister Maria Innocentia's Gift

M.I. Hummel Figurines

Opposite: The drawings of a nun named Sister Maria Innocentia led to the creation of hundreds of M.I. Hummel figurines like this one. The figurine is named "Sweet Music" and was modeled in 1947.

THEY HAVE BEEN CALLED THE WORLD'S most beloved children, and not just because they never misbehave. The innocent, bright-eyed, fun-loving expressions of the M.I. Hummel figurines have attracted millions of admirers and serious collectors. The delicate ceramic portraits of children have been manufactured for more than a half century by a West German company and now command lofty prices. The artist who brought them into the world, however, died many years ago at a young age.

Berta Hummel was born in 1909 in the village of Massing in Southern Bavaria (now part of West Germany). As a child, she discovered that she enjoyed drawing. Undaunted by lack of money to buy proper materials, she used wastepaper and drew in the margins of letters that the family received.

Her father had hoped to become an artist some-day. His dreams had been doused, however, when he was forced to take over the family business. Seeing his daughter's great talent for drawing, he insisted that she get the opportunity he never had, and he enrolled her in the Munich Academy of Applied Arts. Berta so impressed her teachers that when she graduated from the Academy in 1931, they tried to persuade her to continue graduate studies in art.

But Berta had other plans. She felt a calling to the church, and she joined the Convent of Siessen to become a nun. Taking the name Maria Innocentia, she devoted herself to her new vocation but continued to do her artwork. The sisters of the convent were so impressed with what they saw that they insisted she return to the Munich Academy for another year of training.

Berta Hummel sketched this self-portrait before entering the convent.

Unlike most artists, who only gradually gain recognition, Maria Innocentia's art drew immediate praise. Postcards were a popular means of communication in Germany at the time, and Maria Innocentia's heartwarming portraits of children were snapped up by a German postcard manufacturer. Somehow the young Bavarian nun seemed able to capture feelings and expressions of childhood that older persons had long forgotten.

A display of her postcards was put together in 1933. Franz Goebel, the head of a porcelain-manufacturing company that had been started by his great-great-grandfather, saw her work and was impressed. Goebel approached the convent for permission to take Maria Innocentia's appealing pictures and turn them into three-dimensional ceramic figures. Plans for the first of what are now known as M.I. Hummel figurines were soon underway.

Almost fanatically devoted to detail and quality, Goebel required each figurine to go through 25

Sister Maria Innocentia **(right) with Franz Goebel during her only visit to the Goebel factory, in 1936.**

different quality control checks. Some M.I. Hummel figurines consisted of as many as 39 molded parts. Each part had to be hollow to prevent it from exploding under the 2,100°F (1,159°C) heat of the firing ovens.

The first of the figurines was unveiled at a fair in Leipzig, Germany, in March of 1935. As with the postcard drawings, Maria Innocentia's fresh, innocent creations sparked immediate praise in Europe. Collectors began springing up, eager for more of the ceramic statues. Three months later, M.I. Hummel figurines were introduced to the United States, where they drew a small but devoted audience of admirers. During the Second World War, United States soldiers stationed in Germany sent home many M.I. Hummel figurines.

During this time, the maker of these popular character sketches fell victim to an illness that had been plaguing her for years. In 1946, long before the appreciation of M.I. Hummel figurines had reached its peak, Sister Maria Innocentia died of tuberculosis at the age of 37.

She left behind, however, a wealth of art for the Goebel Company to use, under an ongoing agreement with the convent. Even 40 years after her death, the porcelain manufacturer had not begun to run out of drawings that could be turned into M.I. Hummel figurines.

Many people want to collect as much of Sister Maria Innocentia's work as the Goebel Company can produce. By 1952 there were so many collectors in the

Controlling the quality of a product is crucial to a business's success. Good quality depends on the product's design, whether the equipment used to make it is up-to-date and well maintained, and the people doing the job. **Quality control** refers to the methods used to assure that a product consistently meets the desired level of quality.

Many of the drawings on which M.I. Hummel figurines are based were originally published as holiday cards or postcards. This drawing was an Easter card.

United States alone that the United States Treasury Department recognized collecting Hummels as an "American pastime," and officially designated the little figurines as "works of art." The Goebel Company set up a North American collectors' club in New York and saw membership swell almost immediately to 150,000.

Like the others in this book, Maria Innocentia profited very little from the creations that she brought into the world. The greatest tragedy is that she did not live long enough to see the public's appreciation of her gift.

The Fast-Food Pioneers

McDonald's

PERHAPS THE BEST SYMBOL OF THE frantic pace of modern society is the fast-food business. Forty years ago, people went out for dinner only when they had ample time. Even at the cheapest restaurants, cooks didn't begin preparing your meal until you ordered from the menu.

Now if you have a few minutes to spare, you can grab a meal at any of hundreds of fast-food establishments. These no-wait meals have become a part of life. It has been estimated that on an average day, six percent of the United States population eats a meal at a McDonald's restaurant!

Most of the credit for this revolutionary change in American eating habits has been given to Ray Kroc, the man who amassed a fortune building McDonald's restaurants around the United States

67

and the world. But the origins of fast food go back to the two men who started the business that still bears their name.

Maurice (Mac) McDonald and his younger brother Richard grew up in the New Hampshire village of Bedford around the beginning of the 20th century. Dreaming of becoming motion picture actors, they left New Hampshire for the glitter of Hollywood in 1928.

Unfortunately, like many people who move to California in search of movie stardom, the brothers found acting jobs scarce, and they had to scramble to support themselves. They decided that if they couldn't appear on the silver screen, they could at least stay close to the business by running a small movie theater.

That was as close to the movie business as they would ever get. The Great Depression struck shortly after they arrived on the West Coast. Neither their movie theater nor any of their other small business ventures were successful. Richard later described their situation as "a couple of flunkies starving to death."

In 1937 the brothers tried to cash in on the latest fad on the West Coast, the drive-in restaurant. Using borrowed money, they opened a restaurant near Pasadena, a suburb of car-crazy Los Angeles. Originally they offered a menu served by a well-trained crew of carhops to take orders and bring the food when it was ready. In this business, the McDonald

McDonald's restaurants provide a service rather than a tangible good, or product. A **service** is usually used where it is produced—a restaurant meal, for example, or a haircut or a visit to the dentist.

Unlike goods, services cannot be stored. Some service industries include: health care services, such as hospitals; hotels and motels; restaurants; financial services, such as banks; and retail stores. The major goods-producing industries, on the other hand, are agriculture, manufacturing, mining and construction.

McDonald's rates service very highly. The McDonald's motto is "Q.S.C. & V."—which stands for Quality, Service, Cleanliness, and Value.

brothers met with success, so they were able to open a second restaurant in San Bernardino a few years later.

The drive-ins continued strong until 1948. That year the McDonalds hit upon the idea of changing to fast-food restaurants. They reasoned that if they could find a way to prepare food quickly, customers would be happier and more customers would come to the restaurant. The McDonalds wanted to set up an efficient system of preparing food without sacrificing quality. Their restaurant would have the food ready for customers *before* they arrived.

It was far too difficult, however, to set up such a system with a menu crammed with many different offerings. The McDonald brothers decided to trim the menu to the bare minimum, from 25 to 9 items. The first fast-food menu consisted of a hamburger for 15 cents, french fries for 10 cents, and a milk shake for 20 cents. Kitchen operations were streamlined.

The McDonalds figured that carhops would just be in the way. Instead, they had the customer deal directly with the cashier. The McDonalds were gambling on a new philosophy that said, "If you want fancy, go somewhere else. If you want a simple, good meal and you want it fast, come to us."

Apparently a simple, fast, good meal was exactly what many people wanted. Passing motorists were attracted to the restaurant's "Speedee Service" sign and the yellow arches sticking through the roof.

The early McDonald's crews were all-male, with each man trained to perform one task.

Before long Richard and Mac were making many thousands of dollars a year selling 15-cent precooked hamburgers.

For a number of years, McDonald's restaurant remained one of San Bernardino's special eating places. Then, in 1954, the restaurant began expanding into a fast-food empire—but it wasn't the McDonalds who were responsible. Out in Chicago, a salesman named Ray Kroc, who sold paper cups and malted milk mixing machines, pondered the orders that came in from the West Coast. Somebody must have made a mistake; why would a little restaurant order enough machines to make 40 malted milks at once?

Kroc decided he just had to see the place for himself. He traveled to San Bernardino to investigate and was astounded by what he saw. McDonald's was nothing but a small octagonal building in the middle of a parking lot. Yet it was swamped with customers who moved in and out of the place in a flash. The McDonald brothers occasionally had to hire security guards to control the throngs of customers trying to get in.

When Kroc ordered a meal there, he could see why McDonald's was mobbed. He did not have to wait for the meal, yet the quality of the food was outstanding. Kroc thought the hamburgers and shakes were great, but he proclaimed the french fries the best he'd ever tasted. Moreover, the restaurant was spotlessly clean.

The McDonalds' system obviously worked. The product was in great demand. Kroc asked the brothers why they didn't take advantage of that demand to build more restaurants. The two New Hampshire natives said they were already making as much money as anyone could need. Other people had approached the McDonalds with similar plans, and they had experimented with franchising locally. But they had decided they didn't want the headaches involved with growing bigger.

Kroc was 52 years old and drawing near the end of his career. A high school dropout, he had tried all kinds of careers, from playing piano for a big band to selling real estate, before getting involved in malted milk machines. But his years of experience helped him to recognize a chance to strike it big. He offered to pay the McDonald brothers a percentage

A **franchise** is an agreement between a company and an independently-owned dealer. The independently-owned dealer or restaurant operates as part of a large chain and can use the name, product, trademark, and procedures of the company or restaurant that grants the franchise.

Ray Kroc was 52 years old when he got involved in the McDonald's business in 1954. He launched thousands of franchises across the world, becoming rich in the process. Today millions of people eat at McDonald's every day.

of his restaurants' sales earnings if they gave him franchise rights. Franchise rights would include the right to use the name and the McDonalds' system in new restaurants throughout the world.

The McDonald brothers agreed, and Kroc set to

work immediately. He opened his first McDonald's in suburban Chicago in April of 1955 and franchised another one in Fresno, California, later that year. Just as he had hoped, the McDonalds' concept of fast food was as popular in Chicago and Fresno as it had been in San Bernardino. Before long the trademark golden arches of McDonald's could be seen across the entire country.

By 1960 the McDonald brothers decided to step back and look at the empire they had started. Their experience with the Depression had left them cautious and they wondered if the fast-food business

Two early McDonald's advertisements

Beginning in 1968, the old McDonald's restaurants—and their famous golden arches—gave way to the new, more modern restaurants.

was just a temporary craze. Even if it were permanent, the brothers decided they had already accomplished everything they had wanted to do in the business world. If someone else wanted to take over the growing McDonald's chain they had created, he was welcome to it. In 1961 they agreed to sell all their interests in McDonald's to Ray Kroc, including secret formulas, trademarks, and 300 franchises, for more than $2-1/2 million.

Had the McDonald brothers held on to their rights, they would have earned the profits that made Kroc one of the richest men in the world. Kroc built an ever-expanding enterprise. From the 300 McDonald franchises at the time of the sale in 1960, the number has grown to over 10,000, serving an estimated 22 million people every day.

While fast food became one of the United States' important industries, Mac and Richard McDonald quietly retired to their home state of New Hampshire. Maurice died in Palm Springs, California, in 1971, but Richard, who kept many shares of McDonald's stock, lived to see the enormous impact of the business he started. Neither claimed any regrets for selling a restaurant chain that has become a household name around the world.

For Further Reading...

Bryant, K.L., Jr. and Dethloff, H.C. *A History of American Business*. Prentice-Hall Inc., 1983.

Clary, D.C. *Great American Brands*. Fairchild Books, 1981.

Fucini, J.J. and Fucini, S. *Entrepreneurs: The Men and Women Behind Famous Brand Names*. G.K. Hall, 1985.

Livesay, H.C. *American Made: Men Who Shaped the American Economy*. Little, Brown & Company, 1980.

Moskowitz, M., Katz, M. and Levering, R., eds. *Everybody's Business*. Harper and Row, 1980.

Slappey, S.G. *Pioneers of American Business*. Grosset & Dunlap, 1970.

Sobel, R. and Sicilia, D.B. *The Entrepreneurs: An American Adventure*. Houghton Mifflin Company, 1986.

Thompson, J. *The Very Rich Book*. William Morrow & Company, 1981.

Vare, E. and Ptacek, G. *Mothers of Invention: From the Bra to the Bomb: Forgotten Women and Their Unforgettable Ideas*. William Morrow & Company, 1988.

INDEX

Words in **boldface** are defined in the text.

ACKNOWLEDGEMENTS

The photographs and illustrations in this book are reproduced through the courtesy of: pp. 1, 19, 20, 21, 23, Dunlop Tire Corporation; pp. 2, 66, 70, 72, 73, 74, McDonald's Corporation; pp. 6, 8, Johnson & Johnson; pp. 10, 13, 14, 16, 17, The Coca-Cola Company; pp. 24, 27, 28, 30, 33, 34, 36, 80, General Motors; pp. 39, 40, 42, 43, The Hoover Company, North Canton, Ohio; p. 45, Arrow International Inc.; p. 46, Library of Congress; p. 49, Parker Brothers; p. 50, Little Six Bingo; p. 55, Cleveland Press Library and Collections, Cleveland State University Libraries; p. 59, Museum of Modern Art/Film Stills Archive; pp. 60, 62, 63, 65, Portfolio Press.

Cover illustration by Stephen Clement.

An early manufacturing scene at a General Motors plant